STOCKHOLM
THE CITY AT A GLANCE

D1229487

Royal Palace

Designed by Nicodemus Tessin, this sprawling 608-room palace was completed in 1754. As the Royal Family now resides in Drottningholm and Haga, the state quarters, as well as five fascinating museums, are open to visitors.
Slottsbacken 1, T 402 6130

Riksdagshuset

Little Helgeandsholmen (Isle of the Holy Spirit) is almost completely taken up by the Swedish Parliament. The modern section, added in the 1970s, is a great example of marrying contemporary styles with old.
Riksgatan 1, T 786 4862

Stadshuset

Inaugurated in 1923, City Hall is Stockholm's most iconic building. Climb the 106m tower (summer only) to survey the watery landscape or book a tour of the Blue Hall, which hosts the Nobel Prize banquet.
See p076

Västerbron

Many residents state that this 1935 bridge is their favourite vantage point in the city. A 300m walk to its apex will reward you with spectacular views across the archipelago.

Central Station

The main railway hub, Central Station has a vast waiting hall with a circle cut into the ground floor, which locals have affectionately dubbed *Spottkoppen* (The Spittoon).
Klarabergsviadukten

Hötorgsskraporna

Constructed from 1952 to 1966, these five aligned 72m curtain-walled modernist blocks catch the eye on Stockholm's low skyline.
Sveavägen

INTRODUCTION
THE CHANGING FACE OF THE URBAN SCENE

Sweden gets most things right: a tolerant society, an envied political system and highly educated citizens versed in fashion and lifestyle. Sure, for half of the year, Stockholmers complain about the weather, but they make the most of even the coldest days, in museums, ice rinks and the countryside, which is easily accessible on the subway.

While the famous 'Swedish model' has faced the challenges of increasing immigration and segregation, stories about its demise are hugely overstated. In comparison with other capitals, Stockholm is a wonder of order. Nearly 200 nationalities are represented in the metropolitan area, resulting in a rich blend of cuisine, culture and creativity. It will diversify further as it expands – the population is expected to grow by more than a third by 2040. Entire new districts (see p072) are being built, and the central parts (even conservative, groomed Östermalm) have taken on a more cosmopolitan feel.

In the early noughties, the city's sleek, white minimalism turned it into a pilgrimage site for the design-conscious. Today, however, many interiors have experimental and altogether more playful undertones. The locals themselves, with their well-spoken English, zest for life and passion for travel, have taken all these influences to heart, yet manage to retain a strong sense of self-awareness. Swedes have an incredible ability to never take things too far, and always seem to be able to achieve the optimum balance. They have got the perfect word for it too, *lagom*, which means 'just right'.

ESSENTIAL INFO
FACTS, FIGURES AND USEFUL ADDRESSES

TOURIST OFFICE
Stockholm Visitor Center
Kulturhuset, Sergels Torg 5
T 5082 8508
www.visitstockholm.com

TRANSPORT
Airport transfer to city centre
The Arlanda Express departs every 15
minutes between 4.50am and 1am. It
takes 20 minutes to Central Station
www.arlandaexpress.com
Car hire
Avis
T 010 494 8050
Metro
Trains run from approximately 5am to 1am
T 600 1000
www.sl.se/english
Taxis
Taxi Stockholm
T 150 000
Avoid unofficial cabs, especially at Arlanda

EMERGENCY SERVICES
Emergencies
T 112
24-hour pharmacy
Apoteket CW Scheele
Klarabergsgatan 64
T 077 145 0450

EMBASSIES
British Embassy
Skarpögatan 6-8
T 671 3000
www.gov.uk/world/organisations/
british-embassy-stockholm
US Embassy
Dag Hammarskjölds väg 31
T 783 5300
se.usembassy.gov

POSTAL SERVICES
Post office
Hemköp
Klarabergsgatan 50
T 723 6530
Shipping
UPS
T 411 7010

BOOKS
**The Complete Guide to Architecture
in Stockholm** by Olof Hultin, Bengt OH
Johansson, Johan Mårtelius and Rasmus
Wærn (Arkitektur Förlag)
The Girl with the Dragon Tattoo
by Stieg Larsson (MacLehose Press)
The Nordic Cookbook by Magnus
Nilsson (Phaidon)

WEBSITES
Design
www.svenskform.se
Newspaper
www.thelocal.se

EVENTS
Market
www.marketartfair.com
Stockholm Furniture & Light Fair
www.stockholmfurniturelightfair.se

COST OF LIVING
Taxi from Arlanda Airport to city centre
SEK550
Cappuccino
SEK40
Packet of cigarettes
SEK60
Daily newspaper
SEK30
Bottle of champagne
SEK700

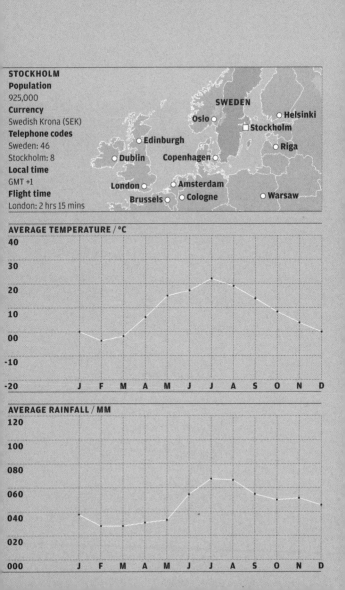

STOCKHOLM
Population
925,000
Currency
Swedish Krona (SEK)
Telephone codes
Sweden: 46
Stockholm: 8
Local time
GMT +1
Flight time
London: 2 hrs 15 mins

SWEDEN

Oslo
Helsinki
Stockholm
Edinburgh
Riga
Dublin
Copenhagen
London
Amsterdam
Brussels
Cologne
Warsaw

AVERAGE TEMPERATURE / °C

	J	F	M	A	M	J	J	A	S	O	N	D
40												
30												
20												
10												
00												
-10												
-20												

AVERAGE RAINFALL / MM

	J	F	M	A	M	J	J	A	S	O	N	D
120												
100												
080												
060												
040												
020												
000												

NEIGHBOURHOODS

THE AREAS YOU NEED TO KNOW AND WHY

To help you navigate the city, we've chosen the most interesting districts (see below and the map inside the back cover) and colour-coded our featured venues, according to their location; those venues that are outside these areas are not coloured.

ÖSTERMALM

Encompassing Sweden's most desirable real estate, manicured boulevards and chic retail avenues, Östermalm is where to check out which labels are in and which are 'so last year'. A mix of yummy mummies, the media set and plenty of old money, its happy residents rarely go anywhere else.

SKEPPSHOLMEN

Otherwise known as Museum Island, this tiny enclave was once heavily littered with military buildings; today it is to all intents and purposes made up of the Svensk Form (Svensksundsvägen 13, T 463 3130) design foundation, and Moderna Museet (see p030) and ArkDes (Exercisplan 4, T 5205 3500), which are both well worth visiting.

NORRMALM

Bustling, central Norrmalm is the capital's business hub. Filled with offices, coffee chains and lunch spots, it is not exactly quaint, but when it boasts Stockholm's largest department store, NK (Hamngatan 18-20, T 762 8000) – the equivalent of Selfridges – then who really needs cute?

SÖDERMALM

Until 15 years ago, parts of Södermalm were considered too dangerous to venture into at night (in Swedish terms at least), but now it's a creative, boho part of town that tells a different story, full of beatnik cafés and bars (see p054), yoga studios and diverting boutiques (see p089).

VASASTADEN

This residential district attracts families looking for more inner-city space – the sought-after properties are in Lärkstaden (see p014). The area is increasingly hip but mostly it's still known for its neighbourhood eateries (see p034), organic delis, vintage stores and stately library (see p026).

GAMLA STAN

Packed full of character and tourists, the Old Town is a maze of cobbled streets and terracotta-coloured buildings containing bars and gift emporiums. Veer off the main strip to discover antiques shops, adorable cafés and top restaurants, in particular Den Gyldene Freden (Österlånggatan 51, T 249 760), serving Swedish fare since 1722.

KUNGSHOLMEN

An up-and-coming residential area, this island provides for the creatives pushed out of Östermalm by rocketing prices. Huge houses have been converted into loft apartments, with a few cosy bistros (see p038) and small galleries springing up on these otherwise quiet streets.

DJURGÅRDEN

The verdant, secluded island of Djurgården is the city's oasis. Within the wooded park are a funfair, museums and restaurants; try the canalside Djurgårdsbrunn (T 624 2200). The path beside the water, shaded by trees, certainly makes a case for being one of the best jogging routes in the world.

LANDMARKS

THE SHAPE OF THE CITY SKYLINE

Alongside the canvases and photographs lining the walls of the Moderna Museet (see p030) are large rectangular windows that reveal breathtaking snapshots of Stockholm's harbour. In other words, for the Swedes, a landscape view is just as beautiful as any work of art. Then again, given that the city is built on 14 islands and a series of 30,000 smaller ones in the archipelago beyond, it is not surprising that it casts a pretty picture. Separated only by a short walk over one of 57 bridges, each of the main islands has its own character. Norrmalm has a buzzy, inner-urban feel, whereas the Old Town, just a stop away on the subway, is all picturesque cobbled streets and homely cafés. Östermalm, which is a crammed residential and shopping area, is very different from lush, green Djurgården, but lies just a quick skip over Djurgårdsbron.

The cityscape is so dominated by the water that any manmade creations tend to take second place, although Kaknästornet (see p012), the telecoms tower, can be viewed from almost anywhere. Newer structures, such as the giant golf ball-like Ericsson Globe (Globentorget 2, T 600 9100), which at 110m in diameter is the largest spherical building in the world, and Stockholm Waterfront (overleaf) sit comfortably in the overall panorama. Peter Celsing's 1974 Kulturhuset (Sergels Torg, T 5062 0212), located slap bang in the centre, is perhaps the ideal landmark by which to navigate. *For full addresses, see Resources.*

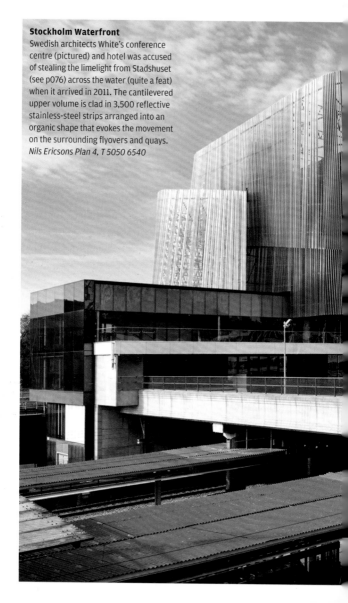

Stockholm Waterfront
Swedish architects White's conference centre (pictured) and hotel was accused of stealing the limelight from Stadshuset (see p076) across the water (quite a feat) when it arrived in 2011. The cantilevered upper volume is clad in 3,500 reflective stainless-steel strips arranged into an organic shape that evokes the movement on the surrounding flyovers and quays.
Nils Ericsons Plan 4, T 5050 6540

Kaknästornet

Known as the central 'spider' in the web of Sweden's TV and radio networks, this 155m-high brutalist mast, which rises out of a wood, bears little resemblance to an arachnid. It was drawn up by architects Bengt Lindroos and Hans Borgström, took four years to build and was inaugurated in 1967. Supported on 72 steel piles driven deep into the rock, the concrete tower is distinctive for a series of four protruding 45-degree-angle platforms festooned with satellite dishes three-quarters of the way up, and a cantilevered crown with glinting gold windows that houses a bar/ restaurant (closed in 2018 for security reasons) with panoramas that stretch for 60km. Detailed reliefs in the facade illustrate patterns of electromagnetic waves. On certain dates, it is colourfully lit up with LEDs at night.
Mörka Kroken 28-30, www.kaknastornet.se

Wenner-Gren Center

Swedish businessman and philanthropist Axel Wenner-Gren provided the funding for this scientific research centre, which was completed in 1962, the year after his death. Designed by Sune Lindström and Alf Bydén, it is composed of two volumes that complement each other well. The 74m high-rise, which is named 'Pylon', remains one of the tallest buildings in the country, and houses a variety of foundations that support and foster international exchange and cooperation. The renovated interior of the top floor has genuine *Mad Men* styling, thanks to Arne Jacobsen's 'Swan' chairs, string shelves and custom furniture. A far lower expansive circular structure called 'Helicon' (visible in the background, above right) annexes the lower levels of the tower. It provides housing for visiting researchers. *Sveavägen 166, www.swgc.org*

Engelbrektskyrkan

Perched high up on a rocky outcrop, the 1914 Engelbrekts church towers over the Lärkstaden district, which is characterised by swathes of red-brick housing dating from the early 20th century. It's the result of a contest won by Lars Israel Wahlman in 1906, at a time when the local population was growing quickly and places of worship were in high demand, and the design is a combination of Swedish art nouveau and National Romantic styles, which favoured the use of natural materials. Take a seat on one of the oak pews to appreciate the 32m vaulted ceiling – it's the tallest of its kind in Scandinavia. Wahlman collaborated with some of the top artists of the era; there are paintings by Olle Hjortzberg, reliefs by Tore Strindberg and frescoes by Filip Månsson. *Östermalmsgatan 20b, T 406 9800, www.svenskakyrkan.se/engelbrekt*

Innovationen Tower

The showpiece and calling card of rapidly developing Hagastaden (see p072), this is the first of two residential towers by OMA, completed in 2018, that offer the loftiest living spaces in the city. The neobrutalist skyscraper has a stepped profile as it rises 125m, and the protruding living rooms with panoramic windows, and recessed terraces, not only give it personality, but also draw in air. There's character too in the ribbed facade, which has a subtle sheen that only becomes apparent up close: the precast concrete was inset with coloured pebbles to create a terrazzo effect. The apartments have unusually high ceilings for a building of this nature to compensate for the lack of daylight in the Swedish winter. Helix Tower will be almost a mirror image but slightly smaller – it will top out at 110m in 2020. *Torsplan 8, www.norratornen.se*

HOTELS

WHERE TO STAY AND WHICH ROOMS TO BOOK

In the past decade, a boom in tourism and the economy has led to a series of notable openings, from At Six (opposite) and its funky little sister Hobo (Brunkebergstorg 4, T 5788 2700), an exercise in collaboration by Berlin's Studio Aisslinger that celebrates local art and design, to the more stately, serene Bank (see p020). Meanwhile, impeccable service and regular updates have kept the established names fresh – the opulent Grand (Södra Blasieholmshamnen 8, T 679 3500) swallowed up Burmanska Palace back in 2006, and was renovated again in 2018. The Nordic Light (see p023) also had an impressive overhaul, and hip Berns (Näckströmsgatan 8, T 5663 2200) has matured since forging its reputation with its celebrity-filled club, and had a makeover in 2015 to ensure its looks don't fade.

While previously the focus was on the business traveller, and hence a sleek, slightly impersonal look, these days the boutique hotel reigns supreme. You can choose from Miss Clara (see p019); Lydmar (Södra Blasieholmshamnen 2, T 223 160), which has an enviable setting, very spacious rooms and a happening restaurant and bar; Story (Riddargatan 6, T 5450 3940), a bohemian mix of downtown New York and Parisian salon; and Ett Hem (see p018), a favourite of those seeking seclusion. If you prefer an even quieter location, but still within walking distance of the centre, check in to Skeppsholmen (see p022), where the sea views are unsurpassed. *For full addresses and room rates, see Resources.*

At Six

Universal Design Studio transformed this hulking brutalist 1977 office block into a moody and masculine-looking 343-key hotel in 2017. Polished public spaces have been fitted out with granite, marble and blackened steel in an overarching palette of warm greys, with furniture by Patricia Urquiola and glass pieces by Carina Seth Andersson. A highly impressive, extensive art collection is curated by Sune Nordgren; it includes work by Olafur Eliasson, Julian Opie and Jaume Plensa, whose 2.5m-high marble head *Mar Whispering* guards the entrance. Rooms (Suite 1301, above) have many bespoke items, from lighting by Rubn to leather headboards by Pronova. Relax at the brasserie, the wine lounge or cocktail bar, or the funky neighbouring roof terrace. *Brunkebergstorg 6, T 5788 2800, www.hotelatsix.com*

Ett Hem

The name of this boutique property means 'a home', and it offers a luxury that larger establishments simply can't provide. The kitchen is open all hours and stocked with champagne and tasty morsels, and you can invite friends over for dinner. The lounge (above) has a communal TV, board games, a cocktail cabinet and an adjoining library, and there's a spa/sauna too. The 1910 brick mansion was designed in the National Romantic style by Fredrik Dahlberg and is typical of the Arts and Crafts buildings in Lärkstaden (see p014). It was renovated by Ilse Crawford, who installed antiques, and art from the owners' collection. There are 12 rooms, detailed with oak, Gotland stone and sheepskin; opt for a Junior Suite with a four-poster bed, tiled stove and balcony.
Sköldungagatan 2, T 200 590,
www.etthem.se

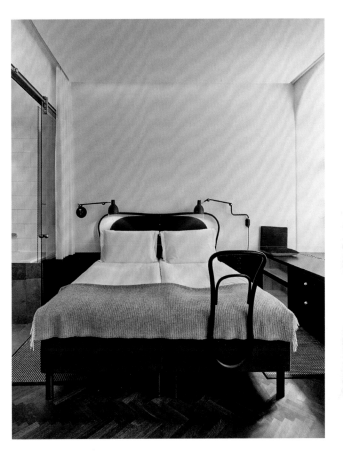

Miss Clara

Housed in a girls' school that operated from 1910 until WWII, this elegant hotel derives its name from the much-loved former head. The art nouveau building was converted by architect Gert Wingårdh and retains much of the feeling from that era, particularly in its long corridors, high ceilings, stonework and wrought-iron staircase. The 92 rooms (Deluxe, above) have a sober white-grey-brown palette, dark herringbone parquet flooring, Örsjö lighting, and chair backs at the bottom of the bed, so you can peruse the morning papers facing your partner. The most spacious is the Etage Suite, set in the old prayer hall. Common areas feature Max Modén's photography and Lee Broom's 'Decanterlights'. In addition to the in-house bistro, Miss Clara runs a pizzeria next door. *Sveavägen 48, T 440 6700, www.missclarahotel.com*

Bank Hotel

The often opulent lobbies, imposing vaults and aura of grandeur of old banks make for a superb hotel setting and this conversion is no exception. It is housed in the Södra Sverige head office, which dates from 1910 and was designed in palatial style by Thor Thorén. Relaunched in 2018, it has retained many of the original elements, such as the green scagliola arches, stucco details and glass roof of the main hall, now restaurant Bonnie's (opposite), which serves a coastal European menu. Elsewhere, the mahogany-panelled Papillon bar was inspired by the former director's office. Local stylists Ida Lauga and Lo Bjurulf crafted the interiors of the 115 homely but chic rooms (Terrace Bank Suite, above), while the art curation throughout is by gallery CFHill (see p064). *Arsenalsgatan 6, T 5985 8000, www.bankhotel.se*

Hotel Skeppsholmen

Staying here feels like taking a vacation within a vacation – the hotel is set on one of Stockholm's most picturesque islands, a part of the city that's incredibly tranquil and secluded given its proximity to bustling Norrmalm. Its two 1699 barrack buildings were renovated by architects Erséus, who collaborated with Claesson Koivisto Rune on the interiors. Natural materials, and a restricted palette inspired by the 18th-century Gustavian style, distinguish the 78 rooms (Deluxe Sea & Garden View, above), which have toiletries by Byredo (see p083). Fine-diner Långa Raden (T 407 2305) excels in Swedish classics such as black pudding with bacon and lingonberries, and Toast Skagen. In summer, book a tennis court or simply flop into a deckchair in the garden. *Gröna gången 1, T 407 2300, www.hotelskeppsholmen.se*

Nordic Light Hotel

When the Nordic Light launched in 2001 it was dubbed the city's first design hotel, but the interior was too gimmicky to last, and in 2018 it had a makeover overseen by Bergen-based architects Todd Saunders. The stylish communal areas now feature statement bespoke pieces by local talents. Johannes Norlander's sofa, Mats Theselius' chair, Amanda Karsberg's Tärnsjö leather-upholstered stools and Fredrik Paulsen's Ölandssten limestone-top table decorate a lobby clad in ash, as is restaurant Lykke, lit by Jenny Nordberg's 'Assemblage' lamps. It serves city favourites like rösti with sour cream, onion and roe. John Tong stylishly reworked the 169 rooms, installing some classic Scandi furniture (Carl Hansen & Søn's 'Embrace Chair' in the Deluxe, above).
Vasaplan 7, T 5056 3200,
www.nordiclighthotel.se

24 HOURS

SEE THE BEST OF THE CITY IN JUST ONE DAY

Stockholm is a city of climatic contrasts, as temperatures can fall to -20°C in winter and rise to 30°C with close to 24 hours of daylight in summer, rendering a total transformation. Equally notable are the contrasts in the landscape, from bucolic tranquillity to bustling shopping district in minutes. These extremes coalesce rather than divide the city, as Stockholmers embrace the milieu with gusto.

As an alternative to the itinerary listed here, you could head to Östermalm for some of Europe's best design showrooms (see p095) and Södermalm for hip fashion boutiques (see p090) before lunch with panoramic views at the singular Gondolen (Stadsgården 6, T 641 7090), or Fotografiska (Stadsgårdshamnen 22, T 5090 0500), which puts on great photography exhibitions and looks out over the archipelago from the former customs house, a 1910 art nouveau building. In the same area, Konsthantverkarna (Södermalmstorg 4, T 611 0370) is a kind of union for craftsmen working in textiles, glass, sculpture, ceramics, jewellery, silver, wood and leather.

Start the evening with drinks at Lilla Baren (see p053). Dine in vibrant restaurant district Gamla Stan, or make a beeline for Adam/Albin (see p033) or, on special occasions, Frantzén (see p031). At weekends, hit one of the kicking spots around Stureplan, such as the apartment-set Spy Bar (Birger Jarlsgatan 20, T 5450 7600) and Obaren (Stureplan 2, T 440 5730), which hosts art, DJs and live acts. _For full addresses, see Resources._

09.00 Sturebadet

The Sturebadet baths and spa complex was inaugurated in 1885 and has long been at the centre of Stockholm life. Its swimming pool (above) was added in 1902 and has a Jugendstil interior by Hjalmar Molin, who incorporated ancient Norse and Moorish elements. A fire razed the structure in 1985 but it was faithfully rebuilt over four years based on historic photographs, and further facelifts have been applied by architect Per Öberg in various stages, the latest in 2018. Rouse yourself with an invigorating swim or one of the 45 or so treatments, which include salt scrubs, facials and full-body Swedish massage. Afterwards, head to the balcony restaurant for a buffet breakfast of granola, yoghurt, scrambled eggs and crisp bread with strong cheese and turkey.
Sturegallerian, T 5450 1500,
www.sturebadet.se

10.30 Stadsbiblioteket

This library is perhaps Stockholm's most internationally lauded structure. Gunnar Asplund's last Nordic classicist building (it was unveiled in 1928) also borrows its forms and ornament from ancient Egypt. A processional stairway beginning at the entrance leads up into the magnificent rotunda, in which you are surrounded by books on seemingly endless shelves.
Sveavägen 73, T 508 31060

12.00 Nationalmuseum restaurant

The dining hall at the National Museum is a triumph of contemporary craftsmanship. Everything from the furniture and lighting to the textiles and tableware was created by Nordic designers and manufacturers. Matti Klenell and Peter Andersson devised the 'Botero' chairs, and the long 'Femettan' table (both above) is by Stina Löfgren and Kristoffer Sundin. Fill up on a hearty lunch of courgette pancakes with roast aubergine or lamb stew with potato purée, garlic and baked tomato before embarking on a tour. The collection comprises 16,000 paintings, sculptures and drawings from 1500 to 1900 and applied arts and design up until today; head to the post-1965 section for classics including Per Heribertson's parking meter and Carl-Arne Breger's 'Diavox' telephone. *Södra Blasieholmshamnen, T 5195 4300, www.nationalmuseum.se*

15.00 Galleri Magnus Karlsson

This small but influential gallery focuses on emerging national artists such as Maria Nordin ('Follow the Line', above) but, with the support of Magnus Karlsson, many of them — Mamma Andersson, Jens Fänge, Jockum Nordström, Dan Wolgers — have gone on to much bigger things. Founded in 1990 in Västerås, it forged a reputation as one of the best ventures in the country and relocated to the capital in 1997. It now represents more than 30 names, typified by painter Sara-Vide Ericson, who came to prominence with her Stockholm graduation show in 2008 and put on her first exhibition here two years later. The venue is located within the 1773 neoclassical Royal Swedish Academy of Fine Arts (T 232 945); its café and entrance hall are flanked by sculpture. *Fredsgatan 12, T 660 4353, www.gallerimagnuskarlsson.com*

17.00 Moderna Museet

In the 1960s and 1970s, Moderna Museet brought contemporary art to Sweden and often shocked the hoi polloi. Rafael Moneo won the competition for its redesign with a vast 27,870 sq m space, much of which he buried to perpetuate the low skyline of the Skeppsholmen docks. He also put emphasis on natural light, and the building is divided into smaller volumes, each with pyramidal roofs crowned by lantern-shaped skylights.

It opened in 1998 and the collection still features many iconic international works. The adjoining ArkDes showcases Swedish design and has an expansive collection of architectural models and drawings, while the gardens feature large-scale sculptures by Alexander Calder (above), among many others. There's a great view of Östermalm from the restaurant terrace.

T 5202 3500, www.modernamuseet.se

20.00 Frantzén

It isn't easy getting a table at Stockholm's triple-Michelin-starred restaurant but it's worth it for chef Björn Frantzén's delicate balancing of Nordic, European and Asian cuisine, incorporating anything from bee pollen to summer truffles and honey cress. Past hits from the seasonal menu include liquorice-glazed veal sweetbread, baked turbot and caviar, and ice cream with tar crumble, whipped ginger, dried yolks and date syrup. Joyn Studio has given the three floors an intimate feel by installing natural materials and a diverse range of furniture. The lounge (above) is where you begin and end your experience, sunk into a 'Bonnet' chair by Broberg & Ridderstråle (see p068) or a 'Dandy Armchair', designed by Chris Martin for Massproductions (see p065). *Klara Norra Kyrkogata 26, T 208 580, www.restaurantfrantzen.com*

URBAN LIFE
CAFÉS, RESTAURANTS, BARS AND NIGHTCLUBS

The culinary scene here has evolved profoundly in the past decade. Traditionally, Stockholmers entertained at home, but these days they increasingly commandeer the urban milieu as an extra living room. Many establishments used to be half-empty in the week but booking ahead has become essential (note that many places close on Sundays). And while it's true that it's not cheap, and the alcohol prices are as scary as you will have heard, in return, the quality is outstanding, menus are exciting, and high-end restaurants often have wine cellars to rival those in Paris. The expense, however, has fostered a trend for casual dining – Lådan (Luntmakargatan 63), one of many gourmet burger joints, serves up juicy sliders and craft beer to communal tables in a huge plywood and concrete box.

What has not changed is the Swedish penchant for coffee, cake and a gossip. Although the big chains have now arrived, the city has a vibrant café culture, evident at Vete-Katten (Kungsgatan 55, T 208 405), which was founded in 1928 and run and staffed entirely by women until 1961. Nightlife is relatively conservative. Bars tend to be quiet until weekends, when the party carries on late, and queues are routine. The vibe is dressed up in Östermalm and vintage in Södermalm. Check out Brooklyn-style bistro/bars Kommendören (Kommendörsgatan 7, T 661 6700), Tjoget (Hornsbruksgatan 24, T 220 021) and Paradiso (Timmermansgatan 24, T 720 6151).
For full addresses, see Resources.

Adam/Albin

In this laidback fine-diner, Adam Dahlberg and Albin Wessman meld native ingredients with an international touch. Their approach is exemplified by innovative creations such as the Swedish taco (flatbread filled with crispy langoustine) and a signature dish of beef tartare with roasted almonds, truffles and pickled onion. For the interiors, local firm Koncept ensured that the kitchen is centre stage; observing the prep is very much key to the experience. Much of the furniture, including the steel-tube 'Jig Bar' stools around the communal tables, is by Massproductions (see p065). Choose the 10-part 'omakase' menu or a truncated version, or order courses at the bar, with a G&T featuring Stockholms Bränneri gin, flavoured with coriander seeds and yuzu. *Rådmansgatan 16, T 411 5535, www.adamalbin.se*

Pom & Flora

Anna and Rasmus Axelsson have a gift for deliciously healthy vegetarian cuisine. The duo launched Pom & Flora in Södermalm in 2012 and added this second outpost four years later in Vasastan. The building dates from the early 1900s and designers Emma Olbers and Maja Lindahl have retained its character, evident in the worn floorboards and wooden wall panels, and added Olbers' birch-and-leather 'Arnold' chairs as well as a gunmetal counter. It's all about breakfast here, which is served until closing at 4pm. Try the house scrambled eggs, topped with fermented carrots, sour cream, *za'atar* and cilantro; porridge with cloudberry jam, skyr and cardamom; or the raspberry and acai bowl. Afterwards, visit Engelbrekts church (see p014) and Stadsbiblioteket (see p026). *Odengatan 39, T 762 496 701, www.pomochflora.se*

Ling Long

Rarely do so many influences coalesce on a single menu. This vegan-friendly eaterie combines Balinese, Korean, Sichuan and Singaporean flavours in a series of punchy sharing plates. Don't miss the mukimame dumplings with lovage, tofu and truffle; snow crab with shrimp, galangal, daikon and watermelon; and fried chicken with roast coconut. Situated in the Story hotel (see p016), its fit-out by Koncept highlights the raw concrete walls and exposed ducts, yet softens the industrial feel with vintage ruby 'Moderno' chairs by Yrjö Kukkapuro (above). The innovative cocktails include wonderful creations such as the Zoelero, mixed with gin, vanilla, lemon, rhubarb and sea buckthorn. In summer, take your drinks out to the cosy rear terrace.
Riddargatan 6, T 5450 3940,
www.ling-long.se

Bar Central

The original Bar Central opened in 2011 on Södermalm. Stockholm designers Uglycute took the quirky eaterie's *mittel*-European menu as their inspiration and mixed Slavic nostalgia with polished Scandi aesthetics. And somehow the mash-up of zigzag tiling, brass fittings, lace curtains and fibreboard panelling actually worked. Four years on, Uglycute repeated the feat here, with extra elegance due to a rich colour scheme. The 'Staple Bar' stools were designed by Lars Stensö (see p047) and the coasters were crocheted by the stepmother of one of the owners. The Wiener schnitzel with anchovy and caper butter is cooked to perfection, and is best matched with an unpasteurised Czech Pilsner Urquell lager from the house *tankovna* or one of the many rieslings.
Birger Jarlsgatan 41, T 201 008,
www.barcentral.se

Restaurang AG

It doesn't take long to figure out what AG is all about. At the entrance, large cuts of meat hang in a huge glass refrigerator, in good company with thousands of wine bottles. Chefs Johan Jureskog and Klas Ljungquist, who together own restaurant Rolfs Kök (T 101 696), took over in 2011 and commissioned Jonas Bohlin to create the interior of this former silver factory (hence 'AG'), which features butcher's tiles, light fixtures from Småland, leather from Tärnsjö and custom-made chairs. Produce from the region's farms is served alongside specialities from further afield, including Black Angus beef and ibérico de Bellota. Game is offered in winter and there are a few veggie options. The signature dish is the dry-aged Porterhouse steak for two. *Kronobergsgatan 37, T 4106 8100, www.restaurangag.se*

Hillenberg

Part of Niklas Ekstedt's empire (see p051), Hillenberg's menu is an intriguing melange of south European and Scandinavian. Hors d'oeuvres include smoked Matjes herring with egg, pickled onion, browned butter and flatbread, and toast with vendace roe, tenderloin, yolk and red onion, while the game meatballs with cabbage, lingonberry, cucumber and cream sauce, and pasta with truffle, porcini and parmesan are popular.

Gothenberg studio Okidoki! custom-made everything from the forest-esque screens to the knives, using beech, Tärnsjö leather and Swedish marble. The graffiti-inspired carpet comes courtesy of Kasthall, and the artwork was commissioned from Emanuel Röhss. Ekstedt's excellent wine café Tyge & Sessil (T 5194 2277) is next door. *Humlegårdsgatan 14, T 5194 2153, www.hillenberg.se*

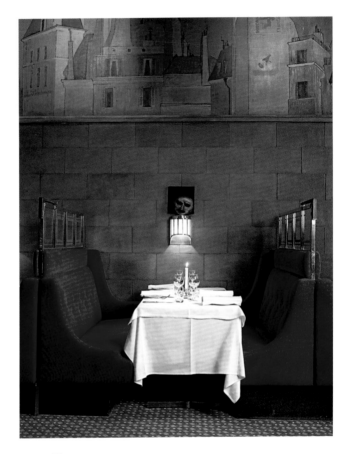

Teatergrillen

This restaurant, with shrouded windows, low lighting, red velvet booths and stone walls, comes as close to power dining, mafia-style, as it gets in Sweden. Taking advantage of its proximity to Dramaten (the magnificent theatre founded by King Gustav III in 1788 for Swedish plays to be performed in their original language), the interior takes on a luxurious *Moulin Rouge* feel, with a collection of Venetian masks and costumes and a stunning frieze depicting a view over the rooftops of Paris. Ask for the secluded corner table 53, order the salt-baked entrecôte with Béarnaise, warm horseradish, salad and French fries, and then see if you can charm your way in to the aristocratic members' club Noppe Bar next door for a nightcap.
Nybrogatan 3, T 5450 3565, www.teatergrillen.se

Gastrologik

Chefs Jacob Holmström and Anton Bjuhr's New Nordic cuisine earned them a Michelin star in 2013. There's no menu; instead, you are served about 20 seasonal dishes in an experience that takes approximately three hours (or choose a 90-minute sequence on weekdays). The highly original delicacies are identified only at the end, and have included razor clams and pike perch with roe and a broth of forest mushrooms and quince; arctic char smoked in birch bark; Gotland truffle shavings and fermented summer cabbage on mini-pancakes; and pork fat noodles with Finnish sturgeon roe. The interior is a blend of copper, leather and wood, conceived by Malmö architect and designer Jonas Lindvall, featuring his own 'Miss Holly' chairs and 'W124' lights.
Artillerigatan 14, T 662 3060,
www.gastrologik.se

Tak

At 48m above sea level, this hotspot atop the Hotel At Six (see p017) has super views and an interior to match. Wingårdhs' chic treatment makes use of brass-and-glass dividing walls, inspired by Japanese shoji, to give this 1970s office building a stylish edge evocative of Fritz Lang's *Metropolis*. The tables with pleated booth collars are paired with 'Lightwood' chairs (above) by Jasper Morrison. In the kitchen, Frida Ronge fuses Asian and Nordic influences to create dishes such as *chirashizushi*: soy-cured salmon with trout roe, ginger-pickled Swede and *furikake*. Above, Råbaren serves sashimi and oysters and the bar dishes out signature cocktails, including the Sesame Street, made with sesame-washed Nikka whisky, maple syrup and walnut bitters. *13th floor, Brunkebergstorg 4, T 5872 2080, www.tak.se*

Oaxen Krog and Slip

Magnus Ek and Agneta Green ran Oaxen Skägårdskrog, a fabled restaurant in the archipelago, between 1994 and 2011. Two years later, it was reborn in a waterside location in the old Djurgården shipyard, housed in a new building by architect Mats Fahlander and interior designer Agneta Pettersson, who were both inspired by the surroundings. The corrugated walls and form are a nod to the steel shed that used to stand here, and most of the furniture and decorative elements, including the wooden boats suspended from the ceiling, are either vintage or constructed by a local carpenter. Oaxen Krog boasts two Michelin stars and Slip (above) serves Nordic bistro food. If there are two of you, order a whole roasted rabbit from the nearby Vreta farm. *Beckholmsvägen 26, T 5515 3105, www.oaxen.com*

Koppartälten

Designed by Louis Jean Desprez for the King's Guards and built between 1787 and 1790, the three Copper Tents are a magical addition to the already dream-like Haga Park. Gustav III commissioned the tents as part of an attempt to build his own version of Versailles but unfortunately the project was terminated after his assassination, and the pavilions are all that remain. Today, the middle structure houses a museum, and in the east tent (opposite), the café devised by Torbjörn Olsson is a masterpiece in aluminium. In winter, it serves soups and casseroles to sledders, and summer brings new vegetables and salads. Also in Haga Park, boutique hotel Stallmästaregården (T 610 1300) lies in an idyllic location by the bay. Its Sunday brunch buffet is superb.
Hagaparken, T 277 002,
www.koppartalten.se

Usine

To convert this 2,000 sq m former sausage factory, a whopping 48 tons of concrete was used – the flooring and walls, the two bars, a 5.5m-long reception counter and a few items of furniture are all fashioned from it. Swedish designer Richard Lindvall has also used maplewood millwork, leather upholstery, galvanised steel, white tiles and pendant lights to create an industrial feel. MDF boards in orange and brown add colour to tables, cabinet doors and menus. Usine is divided into three rooms, anchored by a black iron structure and linked by a corridor art gallery. Swedish classics and French fare are on offer at swish Bistro 38; Envy is great for a lunch of *raggmunkar* (potato pancakes) with lingonberries; and the café opens at 7.30am for breakfast. *Södermalmsallén 36-38, T 1205 1336, www.usine.se*

Woodstockholm

Part restaurant, part design agency, part showroom, Woodstockholm is a feast for the tongue and for the eyes. The eaterie is an intimate 38-seat affair whose two long communal tables engender an unusually social ambience among the often reserved Swedes. Its seasonal set menu is updated every few months – expect mushrooms, game and shellfish in autumn/winter, and vegetables and berries in spring/summer.

The wine list rotates regularly too, and champions small European producers. The furniture comes from local designers, notably Lars Stensö, whose 'Woodstock' chairs and 'Little Wing' lamps (both above) decorate the venue and are sold in the shop alongside pieces by Uglycute (see p036), Mats Theselius and Ploypan Theerachai. *Mosebacke torg 9, T 369 399, www.woodstockholm.com*

Matbaren

Literally the 'Food Bar', Michelin-starred Matbaren is part of Mathias Dahlgren's empire at the Grand Hôtel (see p016). Exquisite bistro fare like steamed pork bun BBQ style and tartare of veal with cider vinegar is served in Ilse Crawford's joyous interior. Also in this paradise for foodies is lacto-ovo vegetarian Rutabaga. *Södra Blasieholmshamnen 6.*
T 679 3584, www.mdghs.se/matbaren

Cavabaren

A fine selection of Spanish wines, and cava in particular, from lesser-known producers including Juvé & Camps and Gramona, and top-quality tapas, all at decent prices, have proved a winning formula here. Local firm Sandell Sandberg's eye-catching interior is another draw, and features its 'Contour' armchairs, leather banquettes and marble-top tables centred around a high-energy bar. The sharing menu lists classics like *gambas al ajillo* with more contemporary dishes such as crunchy veal sweetbreads with mixed mushrooms and truffle. It has enlivened a formerly dreary stretch of Jakobsbergsgatan, along with cocktail bar and rotisserie Yellow (T 362 126), gourmet burger joint Jureskogs (No 21) and fusion concept and party hangout Yuc LatAsian (T 1282 8081), all of which opened in 2018. *Jakobsbergsgatan 21, www.cavabaren.se*

Ekstedt

Chef Niklas Ekstedt, well known for his TV programmes and cookbooks, has created an entirely original concept here, which has brought him a Michelin star. He uses no electricity or gas and has, instead, revived traditional Scandinavian cooking techniques. All dishes are prepared in a firepit or a wood-burning oven or stove, and the open kitchen spreads a pleasant smell of burning birchwood through the cosy room. Smoke and ash lend flavour to local ingredients, and the four- or six-course menus follow the seasons, in dishes like juniper-smoked pike perch, cabbage and knotted wrack. The rustic, modern interior is inspired by Ekstedt's childhood in Jämtland, north Sweden, encompassing timber, leather, copper and sandstone.
Humlegårdsgatan 17, T 611 1210, www.ekstedt.nu

Broms

Anna Broms ran a successful catering firm out of her basement before opening this restaurant/deli/bakery/florist – and it is her delicious healthy dishes that set Broms apart from all the surrounding eateries in Östermalm. The menu, which encompasses anything from falafel to rotisserie chicken and Swedish meatballs, may come across as somewhat inconsistent, but it has proved its staying power. Koncept has given the place a timeless bistro look, with mosaic floors, darkwood shelves and a long bar. It is a fine spot to start a day, with sourdough bread and homemade marmalade, while the cinnamon buns are sublime. Those who can stomach a traditional breakfast of rye bread with liver paté and pickled cucumber should try Albert & Jack's deli (T 611 5001). *Karlavägen 76, T 263 710, www.bromskarlaplan.se*

Riche and Lilla Baren

Stockholm's hottest party people jostle for space in the bijou Lilla Baren bar; this certainly is not the place for an intimate evening à deux. Chandeliers of upturned glasses hang over the bar, there is ornate stucco detail on the ceiling and, if you can see them, there are rotating exhibitions by emerging artists hung on the walls. Arrive before 11pm to get in at weekends, when DJs take to the decks. Restaurant Riche (above), which attracts a similarly chichi crowd, is set in an adjoining 1893 mansion redesigned by Jonas Bohlin and furnished with his crescent 'Tivoli' chairs. The kitchen specialises in Swedish and French dishes, including Toast Skagen topped with Kalix caviar, and birch-smoked duck breast with summer cabbage, plums and chanterelles.
Birger Jarlsgatan 4, T 5450 3560,
www.riche.se

INSIDER'S GUIDE
FRIDA BARD, FASHION DESIGNER

In 2016, after more than a decade at Acne, Frida Bard took the helm at Hope (Smålandsgatan 14, T 709 623 179), a brand known for its tailored garments with a unisex appeal. She has lived in Stockholm since the 1990s. 'It's uncomplicated. Everything is accessible, from culture to nature.' She lives on Södermalm and spends much of her time there. 'Restaurants and bars have launched but it's still rough, in a nice way.' On Saturday she suggests a brunch of avocado toast at Greasy Spoon (Tjärhovsgatan 19, T 722 642 097) before hitting the shops – Sneakersnstuff (Åsögatan 124, T 743 0322), ATP Atelier (see p090), Afroart (Hornsgatan 58, T 642 5095) for fabrics, and Tambur (Folkungagatan 85, T 704 2820) for interior design.

Her office is located in the Industricentralen gallery cluster (see p056), which is a source of constant inspiration, and she also checks out the shows at nearby Loyal Gallery (Odengatan 3, T 680 7711), and Andréhn-Schiptjenko (Artillerigatan 40, T 612 0075). After work, she likes Konstnärsbaren (Smålandsgatan 7, T 679 6032), an institution which draws an arty crowd with its home cooking, and 'super-cosy' Trattoria Montanari (Grev Turegatan 56, T 660 7694).

On warm weekends, she may head out to Artipelag (see p060). Or go for drinks at 'the city's best outdoor hangout' Bleck (Katarina Bangata 68, T 666 1234), pizza at Bistro Bananas (Skånegatan 47) and finish up at Babylon (Björns Trädgårdsgränd 4, T 640 8083). *For full addresses, see Resources.*

ART AND DESIGN
GALLERIES, STUDIOS AND PUBLIC SPACES

The awakening of Swedish art was at the turn of the 20th century, when painters Anders Zorn and Carl Larsson created their famous canvases depicting daily life. They were followed by sculptor Carl Milles, and the dreamy surrealism of Nils Dardel. The past decade has witnessed a new-found confidence, and work by artists such as Mamma Andersson and Jockum Nordström is shown abroad.

What is most impressive about Stockholm is the sheer number and size of unmissable private ventures like Artipelag (see p060). They open often in Industricentralen, architect Ragnar Östberg's 1937 red-brick-tiled complex, which hosts joint vernissages. Here, Galleri Andersson/Sandström (Hudiksvallsgatan 6, T 324 990) and Galerie Nordenhake (No 8, T 211 892) put on museum-quality shows. Discover local talent at Galerie Forsblom (Karlavägen 9, T 207 807) and Magnus Karlsson (see p029). Out in Sundbyberg, Marabouparken (see p070) is an art space in an old cocoa lab.

Sweden has a noble design tradition, of course – Svensk Form was founded in 1845 and, in 1919, it adopted the slogan 'Beautiful Everyday Goods', which is just as relevant today. While IKEA has a presence in most homes, so do classic objects, from Ingegerd Råman glasses to Bruno Mathsson chairs and Josef Frank lamps. Tour the city's bars and restaurants to see work by accomplished studios such as Note (opposite) and Form Us With Love (see p092). *For full addresses and opening times, see Resources.*

Note Design Studio

Founded in 2008, Swedish collective Note has made a name for itself as a champion of simple and elegant yet playful forms. Departing from the minimalist aesthetic of Nordic style, Note has made colour its hallmark, brightening up interiors across the city: in Hammarby Sjöstad, Finefood deli/bistro (T 643 3420) has a delicious palette that ranges from grey and green to turquoise, peach and salmon red. The 'Arkad' pouffe series for Zilio Aldo takes its cues from architecture (in particular, the arch); the family of cushioned stools comes in various shapes ('S', above) and hues. We were also rather enamoured by the quilted 'Tonella' sofa for Sancal, which was inspired by wine barrels, and the 'Bolt' stool in beech and either copper or steel for La Chance – pure sculptural beauty.
T 656 8804, www.notedesignstudio.se

Subway art

The Stockholm metro hosts what is said to be the world's longest exhibition: 110km of sculptures, installations, mosaics, reliefs, engravings and paintings by more than 150 artists. The idea was born in the 1950s and was meant to be a democratisation of art. The collection has diversified during the past seven decades and encompasses a great variety of styles, from primitive cave painting to high-tech light shows. Solna strand (above) is decorated with Takashi Naraha's surreal sky cubes (1985); Gert Marcus' backlit glass panels (1994) are at Bagarmossen; and the deep red of the rock that envelops the escalators at Rådhuset, installed in 1975, gives the impression that you're descending into hell. Art walks in English take place in summer on Tuesdays, Thursdays and Saturdays at 3pm. *www.sl.se/en/eng-info/contact/art-walks*

Artipelag

Björn Jakobson opened this private gallery in 2012 in a pine forest in the archipelago. It's a 25-minute drive from Stockholm but the best way to get there is on a ferry from Nybrokajen (from May to September). The sleek 10,000 sq m building was devised by Johan Nyrén and blends in to the natural site courtesy of its tar-coated pine facade, wide floor-to-ceiling windows and sedum-covered roof. The temporary exhibitions are often themed. 'One, Two, Tree' studied the potential of wood, 'The Monochrome Symphony' included music and fashion, and 'Bigert & Bergström: Eye of the Storm' (above) brought together the Swedish duo's work on social issues and climate change. Also here is a homewares store, a pair of eateries and an events venue, Artbox.
Artipelagstigen 1, Gustavsberg,
T 5701 3000, www.artipelag.se

Liljevalchs

Perhaps best known for its annual amateur 'Spring Salon', this institution is also the HQ of Scandinavia's Market Art Fair. The gallery was founded in 1916 thanks to a donation from the merchant Carl Fredrik Liljevalch Jr. It was the first to be free from royal influence, marking an exciting new era for Stockholm artists who until then had only been able to exhibit in temporary shacks. It displays contemporary and older art across at least four large shows a year (Lars Lerin retrospective, above) in one of the city's finest spaces. Carl Bergsten's 1916 neoclassical building was considered radical at the time due to its pink facade and lack of ornamentation, earning it the nickname 'the salmon box'. Liljevalchs was given an extensive renovation in 2017. *Djurgårdsvägen 60, T 5083 1330, www.liljevalchs.se*

Sven-Harrys Konstmuseum

This 2011 building, financed by Swedish real-estate mogul Sven-Harry Karlsson, houses a contemporary art museum and – entrepreneurs never being ones to miss an opportunity – luxury flats. The architects Gert Wingårdh and Anna Höglund clad it in a golden alloy similar to that used for coins, and its solid bank-vault-like mass is interrupted by deeply inset balconies. Inside are two floors of display space, a café (T 4284 5554) and a penthouse with interiors that replicate those in Karlsson's 18th-century home on Lidingö. On show is his impressive collection of 20th-century Scandinavian art and design, including paintings by Carl Fredrik Hill and Ernst Josephson. There's also a rooftop sculpture garden. *Eastmansvägen 10-12, T 5116 0060, www.sven-harrys.se*

CFHill

Founded in 2016 before moving into this beautifully restored 17th-century palace, once home to the Chamber of Commerce, two years later, CFHill represents the whole spectrum of the Swedish scene, from the emerging glass artist Hanna Hansdotter to established figures including Mikael Jansson and Denise Grünstein. Owners Anna-Karin Pusic, Michael Elmenbeck and Michael Storåkers' 800 sq m gallery hosts up to three often-playful yet ambitious exhibitions at a time in a variety of media. Gothenburg's Tomas Lundgren recreated old photographs in remarkable black-and-white paintings for 'Forever Someone Else' (*Simulacra II*, above), and Liselotte Watkins' geometric works were shown in dialogue with Sigrid Hjerté's pioneering modernism. *Västra Trädgårdsgatan 9, T 714 4072, www.cfhill.com*

Massproductions

Hammarby quay is becoming an epicentre of design. HG7 is an enclave of residential blocks, each one by a different architect. Johannes Norlander's neomodernist Allén houses studios and ateliers on the ground floor — where you'll find Massproductions. The local firm's elegant utilitarian furniture includes the 'Draft Coffee Table' in beech or ash, the 'Dandy Armchair' (above, left), and the 'Mega Daybed' (right), inspired by freshly baked bread. It's all displayed in a showroom created by Stockholm's Guise, whose raw interiors reference the area's industrial past. Massproductions' Magnus Elebäck and Chris Martin, who founded the company in 2009, work directly with their engineers to ensure a seamless process, maximum efficiency and minimal waste. *Hammarby Allé 51, T 789 0390, www.massproductions.se*

Färgfabriken

Since 1995, Färgfabriken has grown into one of Stockholm's most proactive creative hubs. Dedicated to contemporary art and design as well as architecture and urban development, it hosts seminars, lectures, debates and symposiums on topics such as car-free cities. The 1889 building (above) was once a paint factory, hence its name. The main room, an expansive open-plan hall with a high roof supported by rows of cast-iron pillars, is used for exhibitions: Swedish artist Petra Hultman's 'Bryderier' (opposite) examined reproductive labour, textile heritage and women's societal roles. The organisation also puts on screenings, concerts, dance and club nights, and has a decent café that serves lunch and weekend brunch. We recommend the eggs Benedict. *Lövholmsbrinken 1, T 645 0707, www.fargfabriken.se*

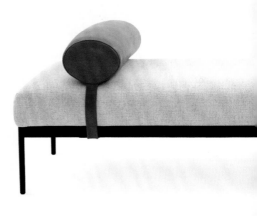

Broberg & Ridderstråle

Stockholm-based Mats Broberg and Johan Ridderstråle established their architecture and design firm in 2006. Their work melds rationality with a dash of wit – witness the tennis-net aesthetics of their 'Wimbledon' chairs for Nola and the curved metal legs of the popular 'Tati' furniture collection for Asplund (see p095). Their daybed for Adea (above), part of the 'Bon' series, contrasts textile and leather upholstery in different colours, and soft shapes with a slender, angular frame. Other members of the 'Bon' family are equally handsome, including a modular sofa that can be configured in various ways. The gold and silver powder-coated-steel 'Pythagoras' candleholders are perfectly transportable. Select pieces are available at Mobile Box (T 442 8388) and Nordiska Galleriet 1912 (T 442 8360). *T 768 556 511, www.brda.se*

Maraboparken

This gallery is housed in and named after a chocolate factory designed by Arthur von Schmalensee in 1916, undoubtedly one of the country's best-preserved functionalist buildings. Today its output remains just as satisfying – local and international artists such as Anna Nordquist Andersson, Miriam Bäckström and Belgian David Claerbout ('Stillbilder', above) have exhibited here, and projects have included a collaboration between creators and local residents. Be sure to visit the surrounding park, which has a collection of sculptures by Bror Hjorth and Ivar Johnsson, among others. The lush grounds were developed between 1937 and 1955 to provide recreation for the workers. Lovely restaurant Parkliv (T 707 156 170) serves a fine lunch seven days a week. *Löfströmsvägen 8, Sundbyberg, T 294 590, www.marabouparken.se*

Erik Nordenhake

Considering that his parents run Galerie Nordenhake (see p056), it was no surprise when Erik Nordenhake launched a similar career, co-founding Belenius/Nordenhake at the age of 26. He ventured out on his own four years later and set up this venue in Östermalm in 2017, where he has since been joined by his younger brother, and represents fresh local talent. Josef Bull's debut solo exhibition 'The Paradise Garage' (above) drew parallels between the iconic New York club and his suburban upbringing in south Stockholm, in painting, sculpture, audiovisuals and found objects. In addition to homegrown artists Ilja Karilampi, Emma Bernhard and Lap-See Lam, US sculptor Stephen Lichty and Vietnamese fashion designer Nhu Duong have shown here. *Lill-Jans plan 6, T 730 498 680, www.eriknordenhake.com*

ARCHITOUR

A GUIDE TO STOCKHOLM'S ICONIC BUILDINGS

When the Social Democratic Party implemented reforms in 1932, public housing was made Swedish architecture's main focus. The city waved goodbye to the neoclassical buildings popularised at the turn of the century by established figures such as Gunnar Asplund and Ivar Tengbom in favour of stern schemes with a functionalist aesthetic. In the coming decades, gaining planning permission for individual projects became nigh on impossible. Due to ambitious initiatives such as the Million Homes Programme that ran between 1965 and 1974, few architects were given scope to experiment, the exception being Peter Celsing and his Kulturhuset (see p009).

Aside from a boom in the late 1980s led by private developers, it wasn't until the mid-1990s, when the growth of the IT industry generated demand for office space, that intriguing contemporary structures started to crop up and architectural practices, including Tham & Videgård (see p074) and Sandellsandberg (see p098) set up in the capital. Now, Stockholm is one of Europe's fastest growing cities with whole neighbourhoods under construction, notably Hagastaden north of Vasastaden, where 3,000 flats are being built near the medical university (see p077), and Telefonplan (opposite), around the Ericsson site, a paragon of 1930s Swedish functionalism. The University of Arts, Crafts and Design relocated here in 2004 and the surrounding housing is mainly in new apartment blocks.

For full addresses, see Resources.

Telefonplan

Before the company moved its HQ to Kista (jokingly dubbed Sweden's Silicon Valley) in the noughties, this vast area was the home of Ericsson, which comprised not just the factory operations but also housing for its workers. Today it's the hub of regeneration of an entire swathe of this south-western suburb. Thousands of homes have already been built and more are on the way; Tellus Towers, a pair of residential skyscrapers by Wingårdhs, will top out at 237m and 177m in 2021. However, the most arresting edifice remains the 1930s industrial complex, now home to a university campus and creative enterprises. At night, its 72m tower (above) hosts the installation *Colour by Numbers*, which anyone can control via phone (T 020 720 200) by altering the RGB balance that radiates from windows in the top 10 floors. *Telefonvägen*

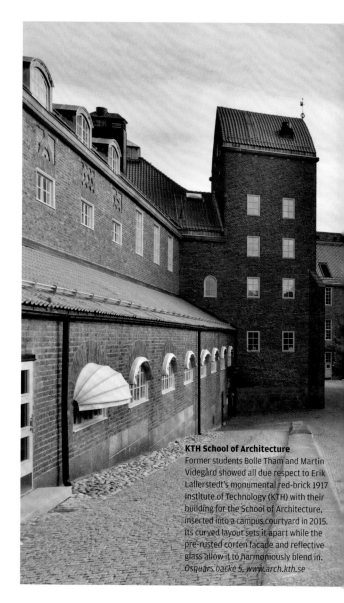

KTH School of Architecture
Former students Bolle Tham and Martin
Videgård showed all due respect to Erik
Lallerstedt's monumental red-brick 1917
Institute of Technology (KTH) with their
building for the School of Architecture,
inserted into a campus courtyard in 2015.
Its curved layout sets it apart while the
pre-rusted corten facade and reflective
glass allow it to harmoniously blend in.
Osquars backe 5, www.arch.kth.se

Stadshuset

Perhaps Stockholm's most iconic building, City Hall was commissioned in 1907 when Swedish architect Ragnar Östberg won the open contest. However, its construction took years, during which time Östberg continually altered his initial design, and it didn't open until 1923. Indeed, The Blue Hall (above) never received the blue tiles of the original plan, although it did keep the name. Today, it is the most exclusive ballroom in the city, and hosts state visits as well as the glittering annual Nobel Prize ceremony. The organ here is the largest in Scandinavia, comprising 10,270 pipes. From the inner courtyard, you can climb the narrow staircases of the tower, which opens from May to September. At 106m high, it provides breathtaking views. *Hantverkargatan 1, T 5082 9058, www.stockholm.se/cityhall*

Aula Medica, Karolinska Institutet

This lecture hall and office complex at the eastern end of the medical university would appear to defy gravity as it hovers over Solnavägen. Architects Wingårdhs were tasked with creating a building wider than the plot itself, and established the formula through a glued laminated timber structure, which is clad in 6,000 triangular glass panes in six shades of gold, white and yellow, and this produces a beautiful play of light inside. Each of the seven floors is larger than the one below, resulting in a soft, rounded form; at its greatest, the angle of incline is 33 degrees. The 1,000-seat auditorium is one of the largest in the country, and is built entirely without supporting pillars. Completed in 2013, it is utilised for major events, including the Nobel Prize lecture series.

Nobels väg 6, T 5248 0000, www.ki.se

Markuskyrkan

Sigurd Lewerentz's geometric, undulating, fortress-like church is tucked discreetly in a white-birch grove in Björkhagen. Built from 1956 to 1960, it's one of Lewerentz's last works, stunning in its simplicity and its considered use of materials. He requested only dark-red brick – to be left uncut – and shunned window frames or door casings to avoid disturbing the whole. The crypt-like nave receives a single shaft of light from a window high on the southern wall below the vaulted ceiling. Equally restrained and moving is Lewerentz and Gunnar Asplund's cemetery, Skogskyrkogården (T 5083 1730), constructed between 1917 and 1940. Three chapels are delicately placed within a sparse pine forest and have sweeping, open views. It is a truly cerebral landscape. *Malmövägen 51, T 5058 1501, www.svenskakyrkan.se*

SHOPS

THE BEST RETAIL THERAPY AND WHAT TO BUY

Nordic design has undergone a renaissance in the past two decades, with Sweden being the major player. Following in the footsteps of Claesson Koivisto Rune and Thomas Sandell (see p095) are Anna Kraitz, Monica Förster and Broberg & Ridderstråle (see p068). Most of Stockholm's prominent showrooms are within walking distance of each other. Svenskt Tenn's refurbished flagship (Strandvägen 5, T 670 1600), Asplund (see p095) and vintage emporium Modernity (Sibyllegatan 6, T 208 025) are a great introduction. There is a healthy independent scene too – visit set designer Johan Svenson's store Fablab (Bondegatan 7, T 4205 1637; Thursdays to Sundays) for home decor, lighting and wallpaper, and Nutida Svenskt Silver (Västmannagatan 49, T 874 8968), run by a collective of artisans.

The high street here, while not exactly groundbreaking, is hard to beat. Local brands such as Acne (Norrmalmstorg 2, T 611 6411) and Filippa K (Grev Turegatan 18, T 5458 8888), which embodies minimalism and luxe fabrication, have made waves internationally, though are cheaper when buying in krona. Less well known is the covetable mens and womenswear at Our Legacy (see p084) and the laidback refinement of Rodebjer (see p086). Södermalm has several tempting diversions, among them Stutterheim (see p089) and Nitty Gritty (Krukmakargatan 24-26, T 658 2440), which stocks Swedish and global labels in a fanciful interior.

For full addresses, see Resources.

Perspective Studio

Robin Klang and Ejub Bicic's concept store celebrates craftsmanship and aesthetics, whether it's inherent in pieces by high-end global names, contemporary Scandinavian makers, or vintage items, regularly sourced from Asia. A mise-en-scène might involve New York interiors firm Apparatus' 'Lariat 1' pendant, a Leonardo Vandal painting, a Naga table, Pierre Jeanneret chairs and a merino throw by Leto (all above). The duo frequently showcase work by innovative Danish design studios Elkeland, Hein and Frama, invite local artists including Bo Arenander to exhibit, and often present new collections of fashion and jewellery. There will always be one-off finds, such as a Vietnamese wood tray or a century-old Chinese stool, and scents from Stockholm's Stora Skuggan and Gothenburg's Agonist. *www.perspectivestudio.se*

Eytys

Renowned for its unisex platform sneakers, Eytys launched here in 2014 with just one natty style: Mother, a low-top lace-up with a thick rubber sole, followed by Odyssey, a high-top version, the year after. Since then, it has expanded with several other models, notably the super-chunky Angel, as well as dress shoes and boots, and developed into a streetwear brand, with a collection of jeans, sweatshirts and tees. The label's minimalist approach is aptly reflected in the interior of its 2016 store, conceived by co-founder Max Schiller and designer Axel Wannberg, who were inspired by Japanese postmodernist Shiro Kuramata and Catalan sculptor Xavier Corberó. Its grey scheme mixes textures and materials, and includes a foam and chrome-spray display module. *Norrlandsgatan 22, T 6844 2080, www.eytys.com*

Byredo

This is an impressive independent triumph in an industry dominated by the fashion houses. Founded in 2006 by Ben Gorham, Byredo's range of scents, some with just five core ingredients, stands out from the mass-produced fragrances. The store has been beautifully thought out by Christian Halleröd and features plenty of terrazzo, in the flooring and a custom-made table (above). It's used to display the intriguingly named scents, such as Bal d'Afrique, which was inspired by late 1920s Paris, with notes of neroli, marigold and cedarwood. Many of them are also available as candles, room sprays and hand and body cream. A further line of accessories encompasses leather bags with silver detailing, calfskin clutches, cashmere blankets and zebu-horn combs. *Mäster Samuelsgatan 6, T 5250 2615, www.byredo.com*

Our Legacy

Founded in 2005 by Christopher Nying and Jockum Hallin, since joined by Richardos Klarén, Our Legacy launched with a range of graphic tees and has developed into a cult brand known for its focus on quality material, tailoring and innovative touches. Prosaic garments are often reimagined by incorporating unconventional details – a sweater with a relaxed poloneck collar, or trousers with an elasticised waist – while boxy-fit shirts come in durable fabrics like American Oxford as well as tactile silk and voile. It branched out into womenswear in 2019, offering slouchy knit dresses, nylon skirts and other minimal staples. Arrhov Frick embellished a stripped-back interior of raw walls, fluorescent lights and exposed ducts with custom-designed furniture. *Jakobsbergsgatan 11, T 611 1010, www.ourlegacy.se*

Alexandra Nilasdotter

There is a strong architectural sensibility in Nilasdotter's work. The Swedish ceramicist grew up wanting to design buildings and her minimalist hand-thrown pottery draws on that same appreciation for structural forms. Many of her pieces are inspired by furniture or modelled after the country's industrial edifices. The unglazed porcelain 'Water Tower' vase (above), for instance, is based on the silos and reservoirs around her home in Skåne. She has collaborated with other Nordic creatives, including the Finnish artist Ida Vikfors, who devised the Rorschach-like patterns for her series of monochrome teacups. Her work is on sale at Konsthantverkarna (see p024). She also runs Normal Object Factory with Taiwanese glassmaker Liu Chien-Kuang; their items are available at Blås & Knåda (T 642 7767). *www.nilasdotter.com*

Rodebjer

Carin Rodebjer's womenswear label offers versatile staples that lean towards relaxed silhouettes, such as slouchy sets, drapey kaftans, culottes, kimonos in loose fits and oversized occasion dresses in summer. The flagship store, in a former bank office, was a collaboration between Rodebjer and set designer Sahara Widoff, who have devised an inviting, gallery-like interior. The pastel tones in Widoff's large pieces of bespoke furniture, including a winding pea-green table and a blush-pink sales counter made from pigmented plaster, inject a whimsical charm, and collections are displayed like artwork on steel racks. We picked up the double-breasted 'Viola' blazer in midnight blue. Next door, Hope (see p054) purveys unisex fashion crafted in meticulous detail. *Smålandsgatan 12, T 611 0117, www.rodebjer.com*

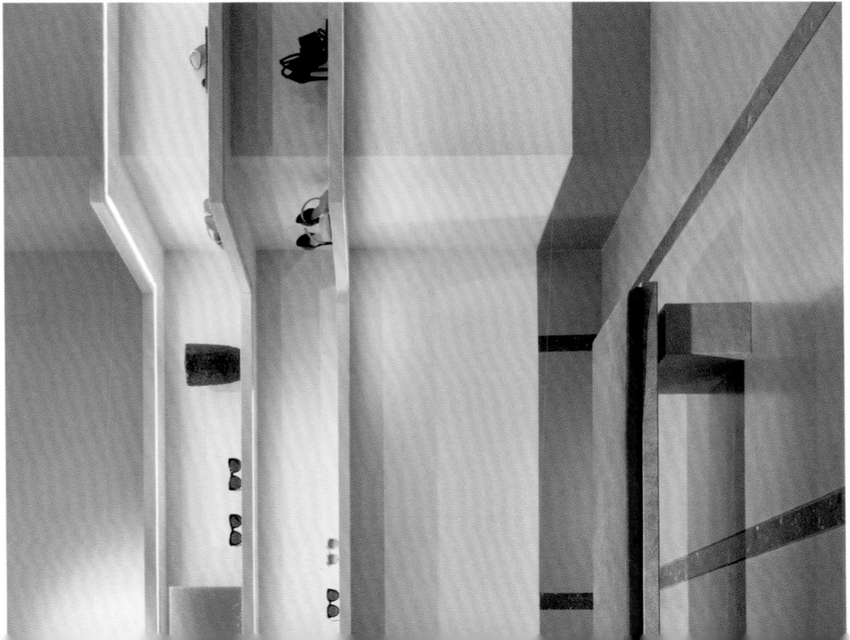

Pärlans Konfektyr

Lisa Ericson's delightful sweet shop pays homage to the 1930s and 1940s when her speciality product – caramel – originally became popular in Sweden. The staff wear vintage outfits and there's a soundtrack of jazz and swing, while the decor features a bespoke oak cashier's desk and brass lights by heritage firm Karlskrona Lampfabrik. A large window affords a glimpse into the kitchen where the treats are made by hand using natural ingredients. Flavours include almond and *salmiak* (salt liquorice), which is a favourite with the locals but perhaps an acquired taste. Also on sale are jars of sauce and Pärlans' cookbook. Everything is beautifully presented, often individually wrapped, in house packaging designs; the retro logo is by Clara von Zweigbergk.
Nytorgsgatan 38, T 660 7010,
www.parlanskonfektyr.se

Stutterheim

Alexander Stutterheim launched his water-resistant rubberised yet breathable-cotton hooded 'Stockholm' raincoat in 2010, based on one that was owned by his grandfather. It was soon endorsed by Jay-Z, who created a limited-edition version. A physical store was inaugurated a year later, and in 2016 it moved a few doors down to larger premises with an interior featuring concrete, steel and birch ply by Andreas Bergman and Fredrik Nyström. Here, the complete range of wet-weather gear and accessories – the collection has expanded to include capes, bucket hats, totes and shoes, for men and women – is on show. Stutterheim also has an online knitwear label, John Sterner, for which garments are hand-produced using wool from Gotland sheep on Öland island.
*Åsögatan 136, T 4081 0398,
www.stutterheim.com*

ATP Atelier

Italophiles Maj-La Pizzelli and Jonas Clason established All Tomorrow's Parties (ATP) in 2011 following a summer in Otranto, Puglia, where they each picked up a pair of simple sandals and fell in love with them. Back in Stockholm, they launched a slow-fashion urban footwear brand combining Scandi design with Italian craftsmanship, using fine leather (vegetable tanned if possible), suede and snakeskin, and the range now encompasses bags, laptop cases, wallets, purses and luggage tags. The stylish store, which has floors of Otranto stone, is fitted out with midcentury furniture and design from Nordlings Antik and art by new talent curated by Carl Kostyál, available for sale. It also carries local artisan jewellery by All Blues and has collaborated with Colovos.
Skånegatan 86, T 1205 5260,
www.atpatelier.com

L:a Bruket

After a decade online, L:a Bruket opened a boutique in 2015. Monica Kylén and Mats Johansson's natural and organic skincare line has its roots in the west coast town of Varberg. And the sea was a key inspiration for a pared-back interior design by James Brooks: the pattern and warped shape of the birch of the lower surfaces resembles the effect of saltwater erosion. These nods to nature promote the message – products that will provide protection from the harsh Swedish climate, such as the eucalyptus-and-marjoram scrub and the broccoli-seed serum. There are also soaps, shampoo, oils and candles. Also look out for local label Verso, whose paraben-free cosmetics come in packaging far too stylish to be hidden in a cabinet. It's stocked at Fablab (see p080). *Södermannagatan 19, T 615 0011, www.labruket.com*

Tid

Stockholm design agency Form Us With Love's wristwear is Scandinavian style incarnate. Watches have monochromatic faces, leather or woven-nylon straps, and Japanese or Swiss quartz precision. Paul Vaugoyeau collaborated on the fit-out, and pine shelving and a concrete floor reinforce the ethos. Another local brand, Triwa (T 701 408 957), is as covetable.
Torsgatan 59, T 820 3380

Malmstenbutiken

Carl Malmsten's wooden furniture is as Swedish as herring and aquavit. He won a 1916 competition to furnish Stadshuset (see p076), and later founded the country's carpentry school. His Strandvägen store has been operating on the ground floor of a 1904 art nouveau building for more than 75 years, and until 2015 was run by his grandson. Malmstenbutiken sells all the classics, including the 'Lilla Åland' chairs and colourful 'Samsas' sofas, and everything is manufactured by Swedish craftsmen. Also on offer here are items by contemporary Nordic designers, as well as traditional handicrafts. We brought home some Gotland sheepskins and a concrete 'Rakkopp' shaving cup (above), which was cast by hand in a small foundry in Tyresö. *Strandvägen 5b, T 233 380, www.malmsten.se*

Asplund

Michael, Thomas and Sandra Asplund have been supplying stylish Stockholmers with clean-lined, elegant furniture since 1990. Offering contemporary classics and special commissions from some of Sweden's top creatives, it has launched several careers, including those of Ola Wihlborg and Stina Sandwall, produced new ranges by some old favourites like Claesson Koivisto Rune, and given birth to beloved designs, such as Thomas Sandell's 'Snow' cabinet and Pia Wallén's 'Crux Blanket'. We were taken by Anya Sebton and Eva Lilja Löwenhielm's white-stained oak 'Palais' coffee table and the 'Horizon Carpet' wall art by rising star Mattias Stenberg. Asplund flirts with the conceptual while remaining a testament to chic and functional Scandinavian style.
Sibyllegatan 31, T 665 7360,
www.asplund.org

ESCAPES

WHERE TO GO IF YOU WANT TO LEAVE TOWN

For all of Stockholm's attempts to come across as metropolitan, you just know that she's a country girl at heart. The city is in such easy reach of so many places of outstanding natural beauty that it would be criminal not to take advantage. Most spectacular is the vast and unique fan-shaped archipelago that stretches out more than 100km from Saltsjön into a magical world. Known as the 'urban wilderness', the area consists of more than 30,000 islands, of which only a few hundred are inhabited, and is home to some of the best hotels and restaurants in Scandinavia.

Extended daylight hours mean early May to late August are the peak times to head out to the archipelago, but winter can offer just as awe-inspiring scenery, when skating and warming up in front of a cosy fire are high on the agenda. Bear in mind that only the larger establishments, such as Utö Värdshus (Gruvbryggan, T 5042 0300) and Sandhamn Seglarhotell (Sandhamn 378, T 5745 0400), are open year round. In summer the choice is much more extensive; perhaps go for lunch at Fjäderholmarnas Krog (Stora Fjäderholmen, T 718 3355). These venues are easily reached on ferries departing from Strömkajen and Strandvägskajen; if you're more adventurous, hire a speedboat or yacht. Alternatively, for something rather more extreme, the north of Sweden has some of the most challenging and well-maintained ski slopes (see p102) in Europe.

For full addresses, see Resources.

Röda Sten Konsthall, Gothenburg

This hulking boiler house under Älvsborg Bridge was built in 1940 as a heating plant for the local factories. It closed in 1957 and in the 1980s and 1990s was used for raves. It was saved from demolition and turned into a culture hub, renovated in 2000 but still plastered with graffiti, named after a quasi-mythical rock nearby. Today it's once again the hottest ticket in town, and hosts musical events, creative workshops and contemporary art exhibitions: group show 'Ingen Rök Utan Eld. Shout Fire!' (above) examined democracy and activism through media including performance, painting and sculpture. Gothenburg is an hour's flight from the capital. Stay at the Clarion Hotel Post (T 31 619 000), which has all the mod-cons in a massive 1925 neoclassical pile. *Röda Sten 1, T 31 120 816, www.rodasten.com*

Treehotel, Harads

Perched amid the centuries-old pines that surround Harads, near to the Arctic Circle in the north of Sweden, are seven madcap tree houses, each conceived by a Swedish firm. Sandellsandberg created The Blue Cone, Tham & Videgård dreamt up the almost invisible Mirrorcube (above), and Bertil Harström designed the equally well-camouflaged Bird's Nest, in addition to the UFO, whose futuristic form achieves quite the opposite effect. The sparse but still sumptuous interiors feature furniture and lighting by local makers like Ateljé Lyktan. Everything from the farm-to-table dining to the two sauna pods works in harmony with the forest's resources. It's a 75-minute flight from Stockholm to Luleå airport and then another hour by car to the site. *Edeforsväg 2a, T 9281 0300, www.treehotel.se*

Yasuragi, Saltsjö-Boo

Swedish workers' union LO commissioned Yoji Kasajima's organic concrete building as a school in 1972. It was converted into a Japanese-themed spa in the 1990s and, after a complete facelift by architects DAP with interiors by Joyn Studio, relaunched in 2018 with 191 refined ryokan-style rooms (Junior Suite, above and opposite). The vast complex revolves around an asymmetric bathing pool and the outdoor hot-spring tubs (onsen). As well as the various saunas and steam rooms, there is a multitude of treatments, classes in meditation and yoga, and three restaurants, including Saishoku, which serves vegan and raw food, and sake and cocktail bars. A garden of bamboo and cherry, maple, ash and magnolia trees, landscaped by artist Gunilla Bandolin and NOD, stretches down to the coastline. It's a half-hour drive from central Stockholm. *Hamndalsvägen 6, T 747 6400, www.yasuragi.se*

Åre

There are many ski resorts in the north of Sweden, but Åre (pronounced awe-re), a 75-minute flight and then an hour's drive from Stockholm, is the most sophisticated choice. In peak season (from December to April), the slopes, restaurants and après-ski bars brim with the fresh-faced, healthy-looking Swedish glitterati. The resort also hosts one of the largest concert stages in the mountains, on which the country's hippest musicians perform. Åre has been dubbed the St Moritz of the north, but this is misleading – for all its superb eateries and hostelries, it is a charming, laidback town. It is similarly glorious in summer, when it transforms into a mountain-bikers' paradise. Stay at Hotel Åregården (T 6471 7800), a National Romantic pile that dates from 1918 converted into a bijou property, with views of Renfjället and Lake Åresjön.

Nordiska Akvarellmuseet, Skärhamn

Danish architects Niels Bruun and Henrik Corfitsen's Nordic Watercolour Museum, located an hour's drive north up the coast from Gothenburg (see p097), appears to float over the water – most appropriate given its contents. Behind a red-painted wood-panelled facade, its concrete-and-steel interior showcases more than 1,000 contemporary works by artists from all the Nordic countries. Exhibitions often focus on popular Swedes, such as Anders Zorn, Elsa Beskow and Lars Lerin, as well as international crowd-pleasers like Bill Viola. Restaurant Vatten (T 304 670 087) specialises in local produce and seafood from the Bohuslän archipelago. Stay in one of the five wooden cabins right on the bay (above) to make the trip truly worthwhile. *Södra Hamnen 6, T 304 600 080, www.akvarellmuseet.org*

NOTES
SKETCHES AND MEMOS

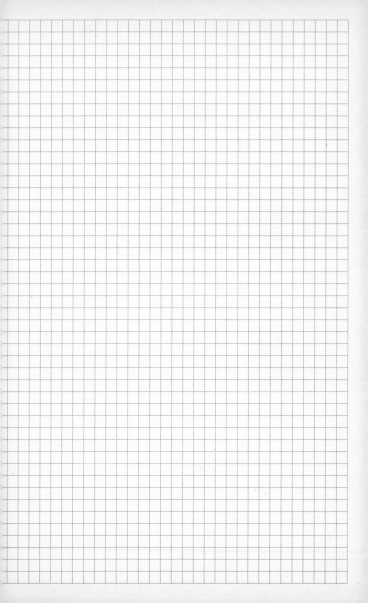

RESOURCES

CITY GUIDE DIRECTORY

A

Acne 080
Norrmalmstorg 2
T 611 6411
www.acnestudios.com

Adam/Albin 033
Rådmansgatan 16
T 411 5535
www.adamalbin.se

Afroart 054
Hornsgatan 58
T 642 5095
www.afroart.se

Albert & Jack's 052
Engelbrektsgatan 3
T 611 5001
www.albertjack.se

Alexandra Nilasdotter 085
www.nilasdotter.com

Andréhn-Schiptjenko 054
Artillerigatan 40
T 612 0075
www.andrehn-schiptjenko.com

Artipelag 060
Artipelagstigen 1
Gustavsberg
T 5701 3000
www.artipelag.se

Asplund 095
Sibyllegatan 31
T 665 7360
www.asplund.org

ATP Atelier 090
Skånegatan 86
T 1205 5260
www.atpatelier.com

Aula Medica, Karolinska Institutet 077
Nobels väg 6
T 5248 0000
www.ki.se

B

Babylon 054
Björns Trädgårdsgränd 4
T 640 8083

Bar Central 036
Birger Jarlsgatan 41
T 201 008
www.barcentral.se

Bistro Bananas 054
Skånegatan 47
www.bistrobananas.se

Blås & Knåda 085
Hornsgatan 26
T 642 7767
www.blasknada.com

Bleck 054
Katarina Bangata 68
T 666 1234
www.restaurangbleck.se

Bonnie's 021
Bank Hotel
Arsenalsgatan 6
T 5985 8000
www.bankhotel.se

Broberg & Ridderstråle 068
T 768 556 511
www.brda.se

Broms 052
Karlavägen 76
T 263 710
www.bromskarlaplan.se

Byredo 083
Mäster Samuelsgatan 6
T 5250 2615
www.byredo.com

HOTELS
ADDRESSES AND ROOM RATES

Hotel Åregården 102
Room rates:
double, from SEK1,500
Årevägen 81
Åre
T 6471 7800
www.aregarden.com

At Six 017
Room rates:
double, from SEK2,000;
Suite 1301, from SEK6,500
Brunkebergstorg 6
T 5788 2800
www.hotelatsix.com

Bank Hotel 020
Room rates:
double, from SEK1,800;
Terrace Bank Suite, from SEK11,700
Arsenalsgatan 6
T 5985 8000
www.bankhotel.se

Berns 016
Room rates:
double, from SEK2,200
Näckströmsgatan 8
T 5663 2200
www.berns.se

Clarion Hotel Post 097
Room rates:
double, from SEK1,300
Drottningtorget 10
Gothenburg
T 3161 9000
www.nordicchoicehotels.com

Ett Hem 018
Room rates:
double, from SEK3,800;
Junior Suite, from SEK6,300
Sköldungagatan 2
T 200 590
www.etthem.se

Grand Hôtel 016
Room rates:
double, from SEK2,200
Södra Blasieholmshamnen 8
T 679 3500
www.grandhotel.se

Hobo 016
Room rates:
double, from SEK1,200
Brunkebergstorg 4
T 5788 2700
www.hobo.se

Lydmar 016
Room rates:
double, from SEK3,000
Södra Blasieholmshamnen 2
T 223 160
www.lydmar.com

Miss Clara 019
Room rates:
double, from SEK1,700;
Deluxe Room, from SEK2,500;
Etage Suite, from SEK4,500
Sveavägen 48
T 440 6700
www.missclarahotel.com

Nordic Light Hotel 023
Room rates:
double, from SEK1,200;
Deluxe, from SEK1,950
Vasaplan 7
T 5056 3200
www.nordiclighthotel.se
Sandhamn Seglarhotell 096
Room rates:
double, from SEK2,400
Sandhamn 378
T 5745 0400
www.sandhamn.com
Hotel Skeppsholmen 022
Room rates:
double, from SEK2,200;
Deluxe Sea & Garden View, from
SEK4,000
Gröna gången 1
T 407 2300
www.hotelskeppsholmen.se
Stallmästaregården 045
Room rates:
double, from SEK1,600
Stallmästaregården
Norrtull
T 610 1300
www.stallmastaregarden.se
Story 016
Room rates:
double, from SEK1,200
Riddargatan 6
T 5450 3940
www.storyhotels.com

Treehotel 098
Room rates:
tree house, from SEK4,400
Edeforsväg 2a
Harads
T 9281 0300
www.treehotel.se
Utö Värdshus 096
Room rates:
prices on request
Gruvbryggan
Utö
T 5042 0300
www.utovardshus.se
Yasuragi 100
Room rates:
double, from SEK1,550;
Junior Suite, from SEK2,750
Hamndalsvägen 6
Saltsjö-Boo
T 747 6400
www.yasuragi.se

WALLPAPER* CITY GUIDES

Executive Editor
Jeremy Case

Author
Elna Nykänen Andersson

Photography Editor
Rebecca Moldenhauer

Art Editor
Jade R Arroyo

Senior Sub-Editor
Sean McGeady

Editorial Assistant
Josh Lee

Contributors
Katarzyna Puchowska
Olivia Berry
George Greenhill

Interns
Gabriele Dellisanti
Giacomo Russo

Stockholm Imprint
First published 2006
Sixth edition 2019

ISBN 978 0 7148 7827 0

More City Guides
www.phaidon.com/travel

Follow us
@wallpaperguides

Contact
wcg@phaidon.com

Original Design
Loran Stosskopf

Map Illustrator
Russell Bell

Production Controller
Gif Jittiwutikarn

**Assistant Production
Controller**
Lily Rodgers

Wallpaper* Magazine
161 Marsh Wall
London E14 9AP
contact@wallpaper.com

Wallpaper*® is a
registered trademark
of TI Media

Phaidon Press Limited
Regent's Wharf
All Saints Street
London N1 9PA

Phaidon Press Inc
65 Bleecker Street
New York, NY 10012

All prices and venue
information are correct
at time of going to press,
but are subject to change.

A CIP Catalogue record for
this book is available from
the British Library.

PHOTOGRAPHERS

Mikael Lundblad
Stockholm Waterfront,
pp010-011
Kaknästornet, p012
Wenner-Gren Center, p013
Engelbrektskyrkan, p014
Innovationen Tower, p015
Hotel At Six, p017
Bank Hotel, p020, p021
Nordic Light hotel, p023
Nationalmuseum
restaurant, p028
Frantzén, p031
Adam/Albin, p033
Pom & Flora, p034
Ling Long, p035
Bar Central, p036, p037
Hillenberg, p039
Tak, p042
Woodstockholm, p047
Cavabaren, p050
Frida Bard, p055
Erik Nordenhake, p071
Telefonplan, p073
KTH School of
Architecture, pp074-075
Byredo, p083
Our Legacy, p084
Rodebjer, pp086-087
Pärlans Konfektyr, p088
Stutterheim, p089
L:a Bruket, p091

Brendan Austin
Miss Clara, p019
Stadsbiblioteket,
pp026-027
Galleri Magnus
Karlsson, p029
Moderna Museet, p030
Oaxen Krog and Slip, p043
Koppartälten, p044, p045
Ekstedt, p051
Broms, p052
Solna strand, pp058-059
Färgfabriken, p067
Aula Medica, p077
Tid, pp092-093

Mikael Axelsson
Usine, p046

Jean-Baptiste Beranger
Artipelag, p060
Färgfabriken, p066

Charlie Bennet
Gastrologik, p041
Riche, p053
Markuskyrkan, p078, p079

Yanan Li
Stadshuset, p076

Åke E:son Lindman
Eytys, p082
Treehotel, pp098-099

Michael McLain
Teatergrillen, p040

Christoffer Rudquist
Stockholm city view,
inside front cover
Restaurang AG, p038

Kalle Sanner
Nordiska Akvarellmuseet,
p103

Tord-Rickard Söderström
Sven-Harrys
Konstmuseum, pp062-063

Hendrik Zeitler
Röda Sten Kunsthall, p097

STOCKHOLM
A COLOUR-CODED GUIDE TO THE CITY'S HOT 'HOODS

ÖSTERMALM
The chicest part of Stockholm, its avenues are lined with swanky stores and grand homes

SKEPPSHOLMEN
Museum Island has all the culture you could desire, from art to architecture and design

NORRMALM
The financial centre is a hotchpotch of offices, high-street stores and independent cafés

SÖDERMALM
Now a slightly left-field district with plenty of interesting retail and hip bars to explore

VASASTADEN
Laidback and residential, this area is establishing itself as the pre-eminent gallery zone

GAMLA STAN
Visitors mob the Old Town for its Royal Palace, cobbled streets and medieval townhouses

KUNGSHOLMEN
This enclave is gentrifying as factories are split into lofts, and delis and bistros arrive

DJURGÅRDEN
Stockholm's green lung is crisscrossed by woodland trails and is great for a summer dip

For a full description of each neighbourhood, see the Introduction.
Featured venues are colour-coded, according to the district in which they are located.